SPARKY'S STEM GUIDE TO...

TRUCKS

BY KIRSTY HOLMES

©2019
**The Secret Book Company
King's Lynn
Norfolk PE30 4LS**

A catalogue record for this book is available from the British Library.

ISBN: 978-1-78998-058-5

Written by:
Kirsty Holmes

Edited by:
Emilie Dufresne

Designed by:
Danielle Rippengill

All facts, statistics, web addresses and URLs in this book were verified as valid and accurate at time of writing. No responsibility for any changes to external websites or references can be accepted by either the author or publisher.

Original idea by Harrison Holmes.

CONTENTS

WORDS THAT LOOK LIKE THIS CAN BE FOUND IN THE GLOSSARY ON PAGE 24.

WELCOME TO
DRIVING SCHOOL!

HELLO! I'm Jeremy Sparkplug, world-famous truck driver. You can call me Sparky. You must be the new recruits. Welcome to the Horses for Courses School of Motoring!

Here you will be learning about some of the biggest and toughest **VEHICLES** on wheels: trucks! If you pass your driving test, you'll earn your Golden Horseshoe. So pay attention: it's time to DRIVE!

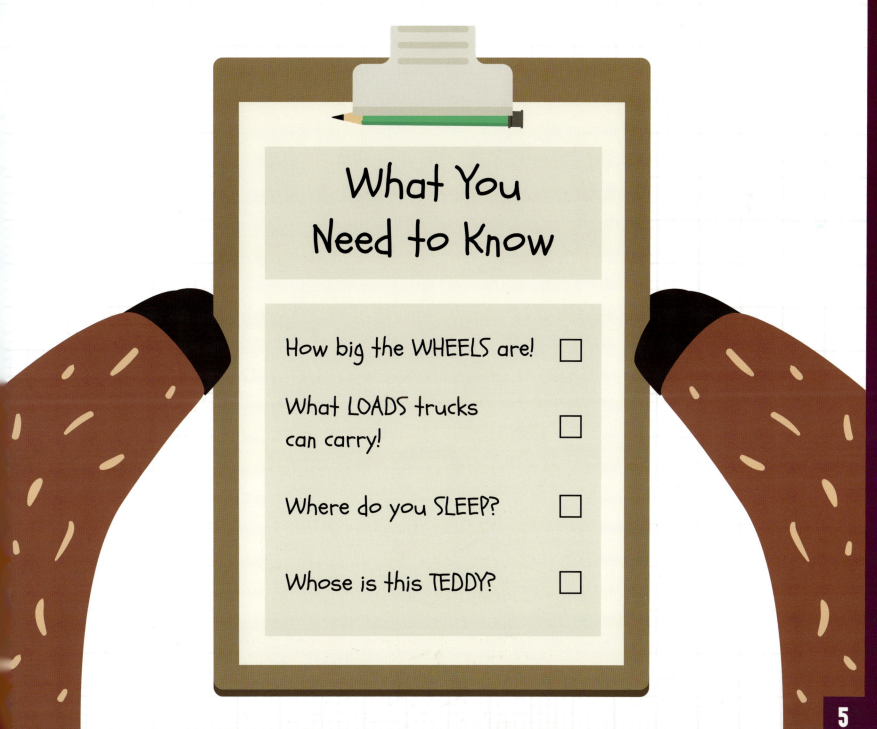

What You Need to Know

How big the WHEELS are! ☐

What LOADS trucks can carry! ☐

Where do you SLEEP? ☐

Whose is this TEDDY? ☐

WHAT IS A TRUCK?

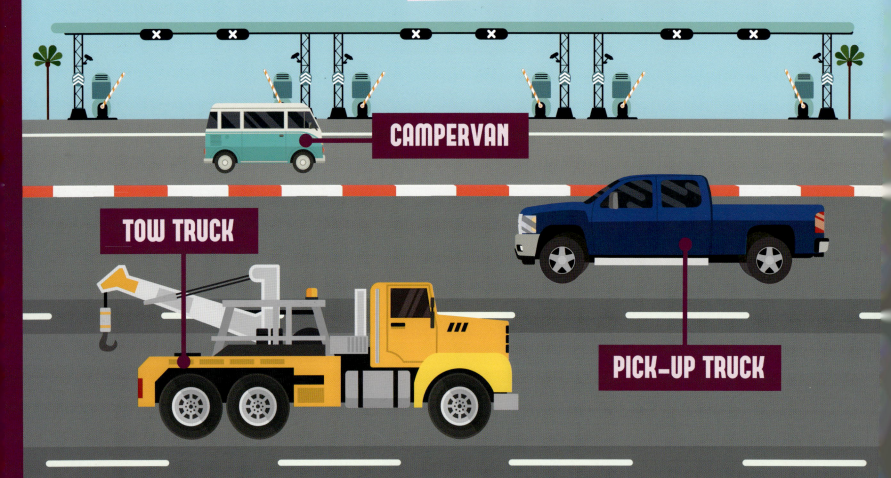

CAMPERVAN

TOW TRUCK

PICK-UP TRUCK

A truck is a type of vehicle used for carrying things. Trucks can carry many different things, both small and very large. Trucks run on roads, and come in lots of different types and sizes.

PARTS OF A TRUCK

CARGO

Cargo means the load the truck is carrying. This is usually at the back of the truck.

Let's look at the parts of a truck.

WHEELS

Trucks can have very large wheels – up to several metres across!

FIFTH WHEEL

This attaches and detaches the cargo and the cab.

CAB

The driver sits here.

TRUCKS ARE ALL DIFFERENT, BUT WILL HAVE THESE SAME BASIC PARTS.

LIGHTS

Trucks have a lot of lights. This helps other drivers see how long the truck is when it is dark.

SUSPENSION

Springs, bouncy tyres and levers help cushion the truck when driving, making it less bumpy!

ENGINE

The engine uses **FUEL** to create energy to power the truck.

INSIDE A TRUCK

SATNAV
Tells you where to go

SPEEDOMETER
Measures speed

RADIO
For top tunes

FUEL GAUGE
Measures fuel

STEERING WHEEL
Turns the truck

IN THE FRONT

Let's take a look inside the cab of Peggy's sleeper truck.
This truck is for driving long distances, so she has to sleep
in the cab when she needs a break.

IN THE BACK

The back of the cab has a little living area for Peggy.
It has everything she needs for nights on the road.

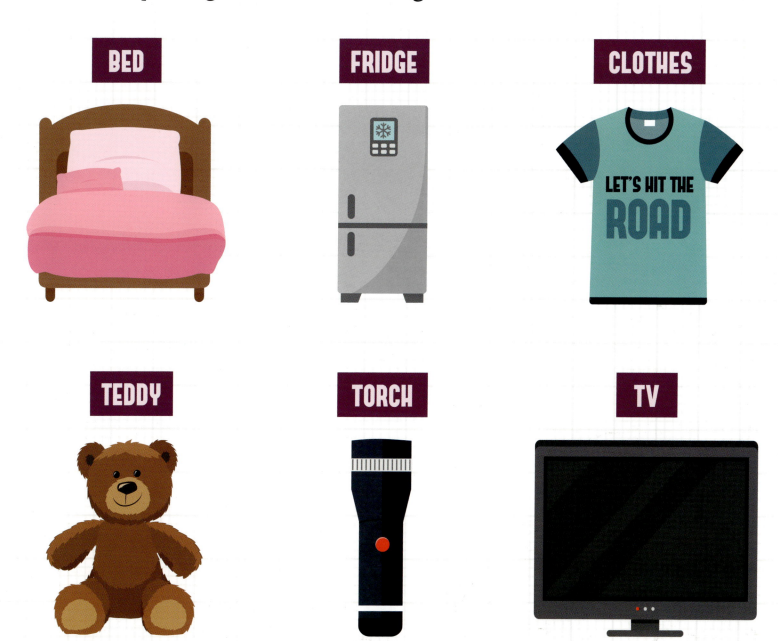

BED

FRIDGE

CLOTHES

LET'S HIT THE
ROAD

TEDDY

TORCH

TV

LOADS!

Trucks can carry lots of different things.

 +  =

MIXER TRUCKS

These can carry a load that needs to be mixed on the way, such as **CONCRETE**.

 +  =

REFRIGERATOR TRUCKS

These have a cold storage area, for frozen and cold items.

 +  =

DUMP TRUCKS

These carry loose loads, such as **GRAVEL** or soil. The back of the truck tips up to dump the load.

Each truck has a different shape and size to be able to do its job.

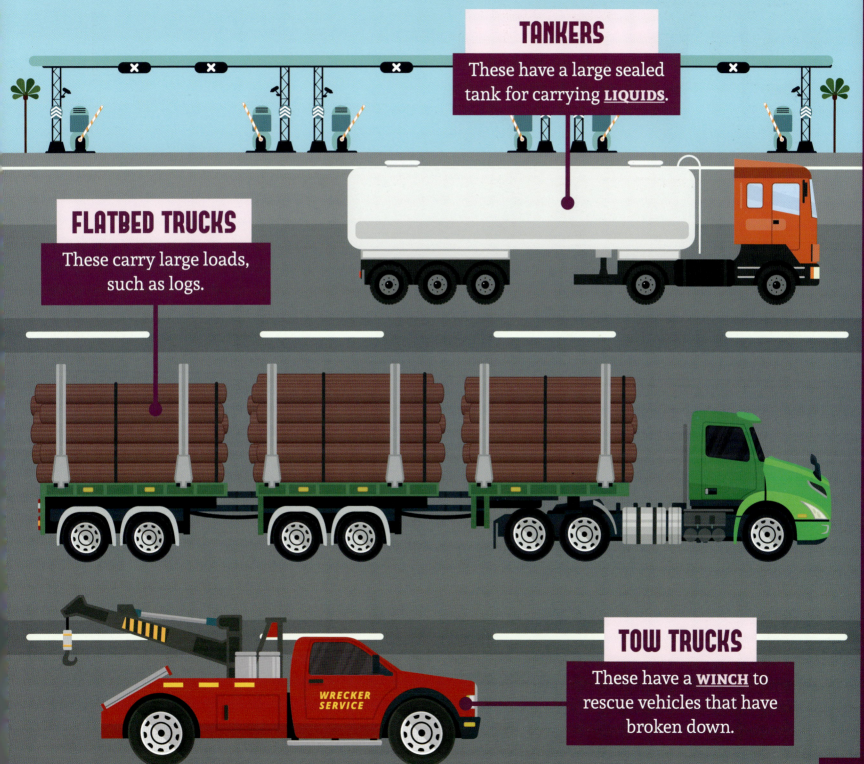

TANKERS

These have a large sealed tank for carrying **LIQUIDS**.

FLATBED TRUCKS

These carry large loads, such as logs.

WRECKER SERVICE

TOW TRUCKS

These have a **WINCH** to rescue vehicles that have broken down.

LESSON 5:
SAFETY!

Trucks can be enormous, so it's important that anyone driving a truck, especially on **PUBLIC** roads, knows how to stay safe.

Take it from a truck driver like me: ALWAYS do your safety checks.

SAFETY FEATURES

NO PHONES

Drivers should always concentrate on the road and not get distracted.

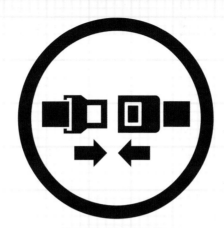

SEATBELT

A strap holds you in your seat in case there is a crash.

LIGHTS

Lights help other drivers see the truck at night.

SPEED LIMITERS

Special computers in the engine can stop a truck from going too fast.

SAFETY SIGNS

Getting too close to a big truck can be dangerous.

TAKING BREAKS

Drivers should not drive for more than nine hours in a day.

LESSON 6:
THE TITAN

One of the world's biggest trucks is the Terex 33-19 'Titan'.

Only one of these huge trucks was ever made. The Terex 33–19 'Titan' was built to work at an iron mine and could carry a load weighing 326 tonnes. Its huge tyres were over three metres across.

The 'Titan' weighs around 450 tonnes!

LESSON 7:
TERRIFIC TRUCKS

SHEEP GAS

The gases produced by a single sheep in one day could be enough to power a small truck for 40 kilometres!

MOST EXPENSIVE TRUCK

The Sultan of Johor in Malaysia had a **CUSTOM-BUILT** Mack Super-Liner made so he could tow his speedboat.

$1,000,000

LONGEST ROAD TRAIN EVER

In **DESERTED** areas, long trucks with many trailers attached can form a road train. The longest ever was the Mack Titan in Australia. It had 113 trailers, weighed 1,160 tonnes, and was over 1.4 kilometres long!

HOGS

ICE ROAD TRUCKERS

In the coldest parts of the world, lakes and rivers freeze so hard that truckers can drive on them – but only if they are brave and skilful. These drivers take cargo to hard-to-reach places during the winter.

DRIVING TEST

Woah there, learners. Time to giddy-up over to the test and see if you're a top trucker – or whether you've just been 'foaling' around!

Questions

1. Which part of a truck does the driver sleep in?

2. What is the satnav for?

3. What type of cargo do tankers carry?

4. What is the maximum time you can drive a truck in one day?

5. What colour was the Terex 33–19 'Titan'?

Did you get them all right?

Of course you did – here is your Golden Horseshoe.
You are now a tip-top trucker, just like Peggy and me!

MONSTER TRUCK MADNESS!

Monster truck drivers crash around and perform crowd-pleasing feats of craziness! It takes years of training, but we're professionals, so let us show you how it's done...

STEP ONE
Get BIG wheels

STEP TWO
Get a crowd

STEP THREE
Get muddy

STEP FOUR
Get crazy!

GLOSSARY

CONCRETE — a man-made material that is a bit like stone, used for building

CUSTOM-BUILT — built specially for one person, exactly how they want it

DESERTED — an area where there are not many buildings or people

FUEL — a material used to make heat or power

GRAVEL — small stones and pebbles

LIQUIDS — materials that flow, such as water

PUBLIC — not private; open to people in the area

VEHICLES — machines for carrying or transporting things or people

WINCH — a machine that uses ropes to pull things

INDEX